CHO

G000155277

CHOOSING CAT NAMES

Simon Jeans

CLAREMONT BOOKS

PENGUIN BOOKS

Published by the Penguin Group
Penguin Books Ltd, 27 Wrights Lane, London W8 5TZ, England
Penguin Books USA Inc., 375 Hudson Street, New York, New York 10014, USA
Penguin Books Australia Ltd, Ringwood, Victoria, Australia
Penguin Books Canada Ltd, 10 Alcorn Avenue, Toronto, Ontario, Canada M4V 3B2
Penguin Books (NZ) Ltd, 182–190 Wairau Road, Auckland 10, New Zealand

Penguin Books Ltd, Registered Offices: Harmondsworth, Middlesex, England

First published in Australia by The Watermark Press 1992
Published in Penguin Books 1994

This edition published by Claremont Books,
an imprint of Godfrey Cave Associates Limited,
42 Bloomsbury Street, London WC1B 3QJ,
under licence from Penguin Books Ltd, 1995

Copyright © The Watermark Press, 1992
All rights reserved

The moral right of the author has been asserted

Cartoons reproduced by kind permission of The New Yorker Magazine, Inc

Additional drawings copyright © Sophie Blackall

Except in the United States of America, this book is sold subject
to the condition that it shall not, by way of trade or otherwise, be lent,
re-sold, hired out, or otherwise circulated without the publisher's
prior consent in any form of binding or cover other than that in
which it is published and without a similar condition including this
condition being imposed on the subsequent purchaser

ISBN 1 85471 768 5

INTRODUCTION

History, literature, sport and Hollywood are rich in cat characters, and in this slim volume we have included the names of all sorts of cats. The selection of names is, of course, arbitrary and concentrates on the historic, legendary and literary aspects of feline nomenclature rather than just amassing a huge list of names. If we have left out one of your favourites, do not give up hope. The omission is probably through lack of space and has nothing to do with suitability for inclusion. The editors are already anticipating an avalanche of letters offering names of legendary cats that we have overlooked, favourite names that should have been included and tales of derring-do by our feline friends that remain un-recorded. We shall accept all your suggestions with good grace and, if this first collection proves as popular as we anticipate, we may consider a second book.

'But when she got there, the cupboard was
bare, and so the poor dog had none.'

Drawing by M. Twohy; © 1990 The New Yorker Magazine, Inc.

A

Abigail A dignified name for a mature cat. The diminutive, Abby, would suit a playful kitten perfectly.

Adam A great name for the first cat you acquire. Also good if your cat likes to sit in the garden.

Adelaide This name originates from an old German word meaning 'nobility', so is most commonly bestowed on cats of the more stately breeds. This name can easily be shortened to Addy.

Aesop Sixth-century storyteller and collector of fables, particularly about animals. His characters are often stealthy or sly, knowing how to save their skins without offending those in charge.

Agatha A sleuth cat named after the prolific author of detective novels, Dame Agatha Christie. One of her books adapted for the stage, *The Mousetrap*, has run continuously in London for forty years.

Ajax Ajax the Greater was the King of Salamis, renowned for his great physical size and bravery. A good name for a courageous cat. Also perfect for the cleanliness-conscious cat.

Akbar Akbar the Great, Emperor of the Mogul Dynasty, 1556–1605. He came to power at the age of thirteen and greatly extended the empire through military genius. For the rags-to-riches cat.

Alba Meaning 'dawn of day' in Spanish and recalls the name of a famous painting by Goya of the Duchess of Alba, who was supposedly his mistress. This is a lovely name for the puss who is as pretty as a picture.

Albert A traditional name, which is now considered dated.

Alfie Short for Alfred, this short and snappy form implies a comfortable, pipe-and-slippers sort of a cat.

Alice In Lewis Carroll's *Through the Looking-Glass*, Alice falls asleep playing with black-and-white kittens and ends her dream journey grasping the Red Queen, 'shaking her into a kitten'.

Allegra (Or, if you prefer, Allegro.) This was the name given to Byron's daughter. In music parlance it means 'lightly', 'quickly' and thus describes perfectly a lively, playful cat.

Am *See* **Si**.

Amber This translucent yellow stone is actually fossilized tree resin. Name your lovely golden kitten for it.

Amy This simple name has famous connections. Amy was the youngest of the four *Little Women* written about by Louisa May Alcott. Dickens's gentle heroine in *Little Dorrit* was also called Amy. It would be most acceptable for the family pet who is of no particular breed.

Anastasia Derived from the Greek word for 'resurrection', this name would be appropriate for kittens born around Easter. Also perfect for the cat born in Russia of royal parents.

Angela From Latin and Greek words meaning 'angel' and 'messenger' respectively. Both, however, seem unlikely roles for the average cat, a factor that probably contributes to the use of the pet name Angie.

Annabel First noted in Scotland but probably a corruption of 'Amabel' from the Latin *amabilis*, meaning 'lovable'. For the affectionate puss.

Antoinette In France the name Antionette has led to a few pet names, the most popular for cats being **Toi** and **Toy**.

Antonia In Portugal and Spain the version of this name is Antonina, hence the very popular diminutive **Nina**. It could be given to talkative cats with sensuous tendencies.

Antony Antony the Abbot is the patron saint of domestic animals (and also patron saint of skin diseases!). His name day is 17 January.

Archibald This name is common in Scottish households. Meaning 'truly bold', it is particularly suited to reddish cats of strong temperament.

Aretha Aretha Franklin, 'Queen of Soul'. Give your cat this name if she can hit those high notes.

Arethusa Greek legend has it that the river-god Alpheus fell in love with the nymph Arethusa. She fled to Ortygia and was turned into a fountain. Alpheus then flowed into the sea and rose in Ortygia and so was united with his beloved. Good names for an amorous cat or a pair of lovers.

Aria Meaning 'air' in music jargon, it usually suggests a piece extracted from a longer work. For a kitten or cat that is a chip off the old block.

Ariel This name is most suitable for a male cat of good breeding. A Hebrew name meaning 'lion of God', Ariel is also a satellite of Uranus and appears in literature as a rebel angel in Milton's *Paradise Lost* and as an 'ayrie spirit' in Shakespeare's *The Tempest*.

Aristotle A Greek philosopher (*c.* 384–322 BC), he is remembered particularly for his work on logic and causality. A learned, serious cat would be proud of this name.

Arnold Good for the thick-necked muscular cat with a hint of a foreign accent – your very own Mr Universe.

Aspasia Considered to be a high-sounding name, it was used more than a century ago as a pleasant change from the Marias and Ellens of that time. Aspasia, meaning 'welcome', was abbreviated to Spash by country folk.

Aster Aster means 'star' and is also the name of a genus of flowers that includes the Michaelmas daisy. There is a variety known as the China aster, perhaps a name for an oriental cat.

Astraea More simply spelled Astrea, this is a serene name for a cat. She was a goddess who dwelt on earth during the Golden Age, and her name means 'justice' and 'innocence'. But when evil entered the world she was drawn up to the heavens to join the constellation of Virgo.

Atticus The gentle hero of Harper Lee's classic novel *To Kill A Mockingbird*. For the intelligent Abyssinian cat.

Augusta For the Romans this name was a mark of majesty. It means 'sacred' and 'venerable' and was originally a title given to the women close to the Roman emperor. Short forms are Gus and Gussie.

Augustus The male version of Augusta and the name given to Gaius Octavius, the first Roman emperor.

Axl After Axl Rose, lead singer of the heavy rock band 'Guns 'n' Roses' – for a wild, tearaway cat.

Ayesha The heroine of Rider Haggard's novel *She*. It is a perfect name for an exotic cat.

B

Baggins Bilbo Baggins was the hero of *The Hobbit* by J.R.R. Tolkien.

Bagheera The panther in Rudyard Kipling's *The Jungle Book*. For the black cat who prowls in the garden as if it were his very own jungle.

Barbarella From the Sixties film of the same name, starring Jane Fonda. Only for the way-out cat with silvery fur who is not desexed.

Bardot Brigitte, the sex kitten of the Fifties. For the pouting, prancing pet.

Barnaby The first person to bear this name was the Apostle, his name in Aramaic meaning 'son of exhortation'. Dickens probably had more to do with the popularization of the name than that devout Cypriot.

Barney Fred Flintstone's neighbour and bowling partner. A great name if your cat's a bit of a throwback to the Stone Age.

Basho An ideal name for a wandering cat, after the itinerant Japanese poet Matsuo Basho.

Basil Yet another name with majestic overtones, this one means 'kingly' in the original Greek. It probably doesn't mean anything like this to watchers of the TV series *Fawlty Towers* who are familiar with the antics of John Cleese as Basil Fawlty.

Bast, Bastet, Pasht The Eygptian goddess of love had the head of a cat and the body of a woman. The Eygptians had great respect for cats, and when one died the owner shaved off his eyebrows.

Beatrice Also Beatrix, both meaning 'bestower of blessings'. And there are many diminutives: Bea, Bee, Beat, Beatty, Trix and Trixie.

Beelzebub In Milton's *Paradise Lost* Beelzebub is one of the fallen angels. He is also a devil. For the cat with hypnotic green eyes.

Belle, Bella 'Lovely' and 'beautiful' in just about anyone's language.

Berlioz *See* **Duchess**.

Bernie Suitable for a wise and home-loving cat, as the namesake is St Bernard, who was renowned for his wisdom.

Bertha From the Old German word for 'bright', Bertha was the name of Charlemagne's mother, acknowledged as a great beauty. For the larger varieties there is also Big Bertha.

Bingo Like 'Snap!', a cry of delight and enthusiasm, and a word to be called out loudly. A winning name.

Blackberry In Sussex, in England, a cat born just after Michaelmas (29 September), which is the end of the blackberry season, is called a blackberry cat and considered to be mischievous.

Blanche From the French *blanc*, meaning 'white', a pretty name for a white cat. *See also* **Orlando**.

Blaze The name given to a white star on a horse's forehead. For the cat with a distinctive white marking on its face.

Blodwin A clumsy-sounding word of Welsh origin.

Blossom From the Old English *blostura*, one who is lovely and full of promise.

Bollinger A classy name for a champagne cat.

Bond As in James Bond – a good name for the cat adept at getting itself out of tricky situations.

Boniface In the Restoration comedy by Farquhar, *The Beaux' Stratagem* (1707), this is the name of a jovial innkeeper and has since become a generic name for innkeepers. Suitable for the *bon viveur*.

Bonnie One of the famous gangsters played in the Hollywood film by Faye Dunaway and Warren Beatty. The other was **Clyde**. For a mischievous pair.

Borgia Son of Pope Alexander VI, Cesare Borgia terrorized central Italy during the late fifteenth century, murdered his elder brother and forced his sister into four political marriages. A good name for a true fiend.

Boris From an old Slav word meaning 'fight', Boris is a Russian name that has become popular in many other countries as well. It will apply well to those cats with a pugnacious streak or Russian blood.

Bowie The chameleon rock star with one blue and one green eye. This could be for the cat that seems to have many identities or one with odd-coloured eyes.

Brahms Johannes Brahms (1833–1897) was a German composer in the tradition of Beethoven and a leader of the Romantic–Classical school. For the cat with a musical ear.

Brandy An ardent spirit distilled from wine or grapes and a name that denotes colour.

Broderick Crawford, a Hollywood tough guy of the 1940s and 1950s. Strictly for the hard-bitten cat.

Brontë Wonderful for the dreamy cat that enjoys a good tramp on the moors and a good companion to **Heathcliff**.

Bumble For the clumsy kitten or cat that does not land on its feet.

Butchkin General Butchkin is the name of one of Doris Lessing's cats.

Buttons The sunny personality of Buttons the cat brightened the dull domesticity of Cinderella's life. Very suitable for an affectionate kitchen companion.

Byte For the cat with megabytes of personality and charm.

C

Cagney Warner Bros. moved James Cagney's date of birth forward five years to 1904 to exploit his baby-faced appearance. For the kitten that never grows up.

Calico Resembling calico material, spotted.

Canute The Danish sovereign who ruled England from 1016 to 1035. Best known for his demonstration of the futility of any attempt to control the tide. For the cat with wisdom.

Capone Alphonse 'Scarface' Capone (1899–1947), the notorious Chicago gangster. This would be a good name for your brawling alley cat who's been in a fight or ten, especially if it shows.

Caprice A tendency to change one's mind without adequate or apparent motive, ideal for those cats who scamper around the house in a world of their own.

Carbon A copycat.

Casanova Giovanni Jacopo, the Italian whose legendary lovemaking made his name famous throughout the continent. Nowadays the name evokes a numbers game involving sexual conquests.

Caspar A salty sea-cat in tales of old, perhaps with Russian ties. For the rare cat that likes water.

Ceepher C for cat, of course!

Celeste A regal name for a somewhat ponderous feline, especially if it displays remarkable feats of memory, as in the elephantine character from *Babar* by Jean de Brunhoff.

Chalky An affectionate name for a white and dusty cat, it could be paired with Cheese.

Champagne For a blond-coloured cat with plenty of sparkle.

Chaplin Charlie. For the little tramp who walks off the street into your life and makes you laugh.

Chardonnay A good name for a light-coloured cat with a smooth feel to its fur.

Charleston Originally an African-American dance, this became *the* dance of the 1920s. For the cat who is light on his feet and loves to dance.

Charlie, Charley The diminutive of Charles, a name used by royalty for many years. Kings and princes of France, Spain, Sweden, Hungary and England have borne this name, including, of course, the current Prince of Wales.

Charivari A French term for a mock serenade, usually after a wedding, made with the banging of pots and pans, kettles and the like. For the cat who likes to serenade you to the accompaniment of rubbish-bin lids.

Chelsea The London suburb that became fashionable in the Swinging Sixties – for a hip and groovy cat!

Cheshire For the pet with a huge grin that brings to mind the Cheshire Cat in Lewis Carroll's *Alice's Adventures in Wonderland*.

Chica/Chico Meaning 'little girl' and 'little boy' respectively in Spanish, these would be ideal names for a pair of cats of both sexes.

Chip One of the lovable chipmunks from Walt Disney. With **Dale**, perfect for an audacious pair.

Chloë From the Greek, meaning a 'green shoot', it was a title given to Demeter, the goddess of crops and fruit. For cats who like lending a paw or two at gardening time.

Chocolate For a tough brown cat with a soft middle.

Christie Agatha, prolific mystery writer. *See* **Agatha**.

Chrysoberyl The chrysoberyl, or cat's eye, is a yellowish-green stone said to have magic powers and to protect the wearer from witchcraft. For the lucky cat with eyes to match.

Cinnamon An aromatic spice – ideal for a warm, brown-coloured cat.

Claribel A more sophisticated alternative to Clare, from the Latin *clarus* (clear) and *bellus* (beautiful). This would be the perfect name for an elegant white cat.

Claude After the limping, stuttering Roman emperor Claudius. For the cat who is not as quick on its feet as it used to be. Or perhaps for the famous composer Claude Depussy?!

Cleopatra The Queen of Egypt who bewitched Antony and Caesar. For the elegant black cat with a striking profile.

Clover A four-legged charm.

Clyde *See* **Bonnie**.

Clytie In ancient mythology Clytie was an ocean nymph in love with Apollo, the glorious and powerful god of the Sun. When he deserted her, the gods in pity changed her into a sunflower, which continued to follow his course in the sky throughout the day.

Cocoa, Coffee Both of these are pretty, if slightly predictable, names for your dark-brown cats.

Comet *See* **Halley**.

Constantia Meaning 'constant', 'unchanging'. It was very popular in Russia, where, as in France, it was associated with royalty. According to Cato, Constantia also means 'cautious'. For the regal cat with a sense of decorum.

Cordelia For the faithful feline. Cordelia was the youngest of King Lear's three daughters and the only one that loved him.

Corinna, Cora, Kora These attractive names derive from Kore, one of many titles given to Persephone. Rowena is another name.

Crescendo Musical term for gradually getting louder. For the cat who begins an increasingly deafening plaint of miaows around dinner-time.

Crunchy A must for the chocolate-and honeycomb-coloured cat.

Cyclops For the one-eyed feline.

Cynthia A name used poetically to denote the moon.

D

Daedalus According to Greek mythology, Daedalus made wings for himself and flew from Crete across the Archipelago; his son Icarus flew with him, the sun melting the wax that fastened the wings, so he fell into the sea. Good names for an inventive, daring duo. *See* **Icarus**.

Daisy From the Anglo-Saxon 'day's eye', for the daisy's petals that close over with the approach of night.

Dale *See* **Chip**.

Dallas The epitome of glitz and gossip and the television series everyone loved to hate. Just the title for a cat with enormous self-esteem and padded shoulders.

Darius King of the Persians (*c*. 558–486 BC). For that regal Persian in your house.

Delilah Good for one of a pair, with Samson.

Denis, Dennis This name originated from Dionysus, the protector of wine, who was worshipped at the grape-harvest festivals. Dennis is the usual Irish spelling.

Desmond A sensible name suggesting a smart cat that always lands on its feet. Can be readily shortened to the more affectionate Des.

Diana An ancient Roman goddess commonly regarded as a moon-goddess and also goddess of hunting. She once enraged the gods by assuming the form of a cat. For the beautiful cat who hunts at night.

Dickens One of Britain's most famous and well-loved writers. Ideal for the literary-minded cat that loves to curl up on its owner's lap while he or she reads.

Dinah If your cat's always in the kitchen, name her Dinah.

Diva For the cat who makes caterwauling an art form, especially at night with an unwilling audience.

Dizzy A good name for a cult cat suited to the Bebop era of jazz. If your tom can play the trumpet, then look no further.

Doric A pleasant-sounding word conveying dignity and style. Doric is one of three Grecian orders of architecture (Doric, Ionic and Corinthian) and is the simplest, oldest and strongest.

Doris Teamed with **Maurice**, perfect for a boy/girl pair.

Dot/Dotty Short for Dorothy and appropriate for a scatty cat.

Duchess A dignified white Angora cat featured in the Disney film *The Aristocats*, with kittens called Maria (who wants to be a prima donna), Toulouse (who wants to be a painter) and Berlioz (who wants to be a composer).

Dusty An affectionate name reflecting darkish colouring. A Texan tabby named Dusty is claimed to have had 420 kittens.

Dylan For an enigmatic cat that likes to sing under the stars.

Drawing by M. Stevens; © 1988 The New Yorker Magazine, Inc.

E

Earl For the puss in aristocratic boots.

Eartha Eartha Kitty, a wonderful name for the cat with a sexy, sultry purr.

Ebony Intense blackness, with an exotic air, like the hard blackwood native to Ceylon and Mauritius. Lovely for one of a pair, where colours contrast: Ebony and **Ivory**.

Echo In Roman mythology Echo was a nymph whose love for Narcissus was unrequited, so she pined away until only her voice was left. A suitable name for a cat who shadows a companion.

Elba Napoleon's island of exile, for the cat whose territory is limited.

Eliot *Old Possum's Book of Practical Cats*, T.S. Eliot's work, has been popularized by the hugely successful musical *Cats* (1981).

Eliza For Eliza Doolittle, the heroine from *My Fair Lady*. An apt name if you're constantly trying to improve your cat's manners.

Ella From an ancient Germanic word meaning 'all', this name was revived by the Victorians but immortalized by that jazz great, Ella Fitzgerald.

Elsa The Old German for 'noble maiden', Elsa has undergone its greatest revival as a name for cats with Joy Adamson's tale of her beloved lion Elsa in the book *Born Free*.

Elvis A good name if your cat likes to croon at the moon.

Emma Emma Hamilton was Lord Nelson's mistress. If your cat has as a friend a tom that is blind in one eye and is missing his front right paw, then Emma is right for her.

Erratum A good name for the kitten that you were once determined not to adopt.

Faldo After the golfer Nick Faldo – for the cat with eagle-eye concentration while stalking.

Fantasia Inspire musical appreciation in your cat by naming it after this 1940 animated Disney film, which gives a visual interpretation of compositions by Tchaikovsky and others.

Farouk Farouk I (1920–1965) came to the Egyptian throne in 1936. His increasingly hedonistic, extravagant life-style led to dissatisfaction among his subjects, and he was deposed in 1952. This name would suit an exotic, flamboyant and very fat cat.

Fat Cat The only name for a cat in the public service.

Father Gotto The wise old cat who presided over all the others in the fairy tale *The Colony of Cats* by Andrew Lang.

Fauna One of the three sprites in Disney's version of *Sleeping Beauty*. If your cat protects the house with a little magic, here's a good name for her. *See* **Flora**, **Meriwether**.

Fauntleroy For most people this name has but one association, that of the little American boy in the Victorian novel who won all hearts. But it has medieval Anglo-French origins. 'Faunt' was derived from 'infant', 'leroy' from *le roi*, the king.

Feiffer For the witty cat, from the well-known US cartoonist.

Felis Our domestic cats come from the genus *Felis catus*.

Felix *Felix* is a Latin word meaning 'happy' and is the name of the animated feline star of countless silent movies of the Twenties. Would suit a cat with huge eyes and an unblinking stare.

Flash For the cat with the super-hero streak.

Flo-Jo The American sprinter almost more famous for her fabulously long nails than for her running – for a cat that's fast with her claws!

Flopsy After one of Beatrix Potter's rabbits in *The Tale of Peter Rabbit*.

Flora One of three sisters in Disney's version of *Sleeping Beauty*. *See* **Fauna**, **Meriwether**.

Fluff/Fluffy For your Angora kitten.

Foss This famous pet of nineteenth-century humorist Edward Lear lived to the age of seventeen. Lear immortalized him in a series of sketches.

Fracas An ideal name for a troublesome cat that is the cause of many mishaps and squabbles.

Freckle If your pet is spotted or has markings on his nose, call him by this affectionate name.

Freya, Frejya The pagan Scandinavian goddess of love and fertility whose chariot was said to have been drawn by cats.

Frisbee For the light-footed, beach-loving cat.

Fum Fum is an unusual name for a golden cat. In Chinese legend Fum was the phoenix born in the Sun's halo.

G

Gabin Jean, a famous French movie star. For the sleek cat who charms the birds out of the trees.

Gable Clark, King of Hollywood. For the fasionable feline who makes all the female cats in the neighbourhood swoon (and doesn't give a damn).

Galahad Reputedly the purest of all King Arthur's Knights of the Round Table. For the cat with fur like freshly fallen snow.

Ganymede In Greek mythology the cup-bearer of Zeus, a youthful male beauty. In Shakespeare's *As You Like It* Rosalind disguises herself as a man and takes the name. So if your tom is good-looking, then this is perfect.

Garbo Greta, the late and great movie star. For the smoky Persians or sultry Siamese that just want to be alone.

Garfield The lasagne-loving superstar owned by the hapless Jon.

Gaylord From Middle English, meaning 'lively' or 'gay'. For the cat who knows how to enjoy life.

Geneva The city in Switzerland that is usually associated with the Red Cross. This name is also connected with the alcohol gin. The Old French *genèvre*, or juniper berry, is used to flavour gin.

George This name comes from the Greek for 'tiller of the ground' or 'farmer'. For a country cat.

Gerda An original choice for a white cat. Gerda is found in Scandinavian mythology, the daughter of the Frost Giant Gymir. Gerda was so beautiful that the brightness of her white arms illuminated both air and sea.

Ghost An elusive or illusive cat.

Gioconda La Gioconda, Mona Lisa, for the enigmatic cat who looks as if she's swallowed the canary.

Gib Short for Gilbert, an ancient name for a cat, especially a tomcat, which later came to mean a castrated tomcat. Chaucer wrote of 'Gibbe, our Cat', and Shakespeare wrote in *Henry IV* 'as melancholy as a gib cat'.

Gibb A cat hauled up in the notorious English witch trials of the seventeenth century. According to trial records, it was said that Gibb had the ability to speak. So if your cat manages more than *miaow* . . .

Gilbert This would also suit one of a pair of cats who sing for their supper; the other would be **Sullivan**, of course. *See* **Gib**.

Gin A very popular aperitif with **Tonic** – good for a pair of cats with a bit of fizz.

Ginger A common name, referring to the colour of the coat, though C.S. Lewis thought differently. The *Chronicles of Narnia* ends with *The Last Battle*, in which Ginger the cat becomes puppet of the devil.

Giza The suburb of Cairo where the most famous sphinx is situated. The sphinx has a lion's body and human head, usually that of a pharaoh.

Gloves A variation on the name Socks for a cat with white front paws.

Gobbolino The name of the witch's cat in the popular children's books by Ursula Moray Williams.

Godiva For a chocolate-coloured cat.

Godot From Beckett's renowned play *Waiting for Godot*, written in the tradition of the Theatre of the Absurd. For the intangible cat.

Godzilla If your kitten's a little terror, then name it after Godzilla, a film monster (awakened by an H-bomb) that menaces Tokyo.

Goldie For the companion who is worth his or her weight in gold.

Gonzo The lovable Muppet with a huge nose who conducts a choir of singing chickens.

Grace *See* **Orlando**.

Greedigut, Grizzel Seventeenth-century familiars named in Hopkins's treatise *The Discovery of Witches*. He claimed that these were names 'no mortal could invent'.

Greymalkin, Grimalkin An old cat, especially a witch's familiar.

Gringo The Mexican slang word for 'foreigner'. For the cat who appears out of place.

Griselda, Grisel This name means a woman of exemplary patience and meekness. It comes from the story of Patient Grisel, the last tale in Boccaccio's *Decameron*. From there it was used by many authors, including Chaucer, who tells of Grissell who endured the humiliations and cruelties inflicted upon her by her husband without so much as a murmur. They do not make cats like this.

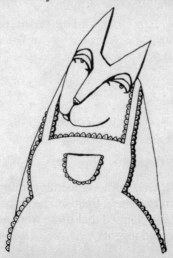

Grizzle This word has two meanings, to complain or whine and also grey-haired. Sound like someone you know?

Grundy 'Solomon Grundy, born on a Monday . . . ' A good name for a risk-taking cat with a short life expectancy.

Gummo One of the Marx Brothers, or perhaps the pet who sticks to you.

Gustav A dignified name, after Gustav Holst (1874–1934), composer of a nocturnal animal's dream music, *The Planets*. Also a name found frequently among Scandinavian royalty.

H

Halley Halley's comet is named after the English astronomer (1656–1742). 'Comet' comes from the Greek meaning 'long-haired star' and has the additional connotations of speed and spectacle.

Hamadryad The Hamadryads were nymphs who lived and died with the trees that they inhabited. As a tree is usually a safe harbour for cats that are being chased by dogs, this is an apt name for most varieties.

Harold If your pet shows leadership qualities, this name of kings would spur him on to greater heights. An irreverent abbreviation would be Harry.

Hazel If your feline friend fixes you with a big green-eyed stare, then this is the ideal appellation.

Heathcliff The brooding lover of Catherine from *Wuthering Heights*.

Hecate The Roman goddess of the moon often affiliated with Diana/Artemis – for a cat that likes to stare at the moon.

Hecuba The Queen of Troy. According to legend, she clawed out the eyes of the King of Thrace and was later transformed into a dog. Does your cat have an evil temper? If so, you could threaten her with the same fate.

Hegel For the philosophical cat who likes to sit back and observe the wonders of the universe.

Heidi The little Swiss mountain girl from the eponymous children's classic. For a cat with a love of heights – or perhaps one with a fondness for 'yowdling'!

Hendrix Jimi was described by *Life* magazine as 'a rock demigod', by *The New York Times* as the 'black Elvis' and by John Lennon as the 'Pied Piper of rock'. A good name for a wild and groovy cat.

Hercules In legend, Hercules helped Jason find the Golden Fleece. The name has become synonymous with great strength and would be ideal for the muscular male.

Hermione A famous British comedienne (Gingold), for the kitty with refined diction.

Hilda A Celtic British saint, Hilda sponsored Caedmon in his literary endeavours. Perfect name for the cat with sense enough not to park herself on your writing tablet.

Hocus Pocus Words uttered by a magician when he performs a trick that usually turns out to be a con job. For the devious cat who pulls the wool over your eyes.

Hodge Dr Johnson's cat. A good name for an intellectual loner.

Holmes *See* **Sherlock**.

Honey For the sweetest cat in all the world.

Hope One of the trio of Hope, Faith and Charity. If your kitten is a terror now, you can hope she'll grow out of it.

I

Icarus Icarus is, in Greek mythology, the man who defied his father **Daedalus** and flew too close to the sun, thereby melting the wax of his man-made wings, causing him to plummet into the sea.

Imelda A fitting name for the puss with a penchant for shoes.

Inca A Peruvian cat would fit the bill.

India Name her after the subcontinent or for the colour of her fur, which is as black as India ink.

Inigo Inigo Jones revolutionized British architecture, adding Italian styles (such as the Banqueting House in Whitehall) to London's drab streets. Definitely a name for a sophisticat.

Irma Name your cat for *Irma la Douce* if she likes to loiter on street corners late at night.

Isaac For the cat who attempts to defy the law of gravity.

Isis Goddess of ancient Egypt, wife of **Osiris**. A wonderful name for the helpful, faithful companion.

Isolde *See* **Tristan**.

Ivory *See* **Ebony**.

J

Jack A wonderfully simple name with many different connotations, such as Jack-in-the-box, Jack Frost, Jack the Ripper, Jack and Jill, jack rabbit, Jack Horner, or any of many famous men, a name to suit any cat.

Jackson General Stonewall, for a street-fighting cat, or the artist, Jackson Pollock, for that creative creature.

Jacob Hebrew patriarch who wrestled with an angel. Watching your kittens tussle in play may bring this name to mind.

Jade Only for the cat with eyes of purest jade

Jagger For a 'Jumping Jack Flash' of a cat.

Jarmara The name of a witch's familiar, traditionally thought of as feline, belonging to a woman seized by Matthew Hopkins, the notorious witch-finder of seventeenth-century England.

Jasper For Jasper Johns (b. 1930) the American painter, or for the stone, which is usually red, yellow or brown.

Jazz For the syncopated feline who dances to his own rhythm.

Jeeves P.G. Wodehouse's superior valet. If your cat has impeccable manners, this is the name.

Jemima For an old duck of a cat.

Jeremiah Perfect name for a cat whose wailings seem to be eternal.

Jeoffry A pleasant name, with added pleasure if you recall Christopher Smart's lines from *Jubilate Agno* about his cat Jeoffry:

> For he counteracts the powers of darkness
> By his electrical skin and glaring eyes.

Joey Pal, as in the musical *Pal Joey*.

Jonah Biblical hero, swallowed by a whale. For the cat whose fish-loving habits may get him into trouble.

Joshua Biblical hero, conqueror of Jericho. If your cat's voice reminds you of a trumpet blast, Joshua may be a good name for him.

Joyce A popular girl's name in the mid twentieth century, which can also be used for a male, perhaps in reference to the literary giant James Joyce, the author of *Ulysses*.

K

Karma In Buddhism/Hinduism, this is the unbroken sequence of cause and effect; a Sanskrit word meaning 'action' or 'sequence'. The perfect name if you and your cat are on the same wavelength.

Kellogg For the flaky cat who loves his breakfast.

Kerouac Jack Kerouac of course, favourite author of the 'Beat Generation' and one hep cat.

Kingston If your feline's fur inclines towards dreadlocks and he listens to reggae, then name him after the capital of Jamaica.

Kir White wine and blackcurrant syrup. For the cat with blonde and red markings.

Klutz Perfect name for the clumsy cat.

Koshka A lovely sounding name for a mooching Muscovite mouser. It is, in fact, the Russian word for 'cat'.

L

Laurence After Sir Laurence Olivier. For a very handsome cat with a love of theatrics.

Leo *Leo* is Latin for 'lion'. If your pet thinks he is King of the Jungle and has a ferocious miaow, then no other name will do.

Leonardo If your cat has a natural creative flair or an enigmatic smile, then name him after the great Renaissance painter Leonardo da Vinci (1452–1519).

Liberty To the Romans the cat was a symbol of Liberty; to Americans the Statue of Liberty represents democratic freedom. For the emancipated cat.

Lily In *Through the Looking-Glass* the Red Queen introduces Alice to 'My precious Lily! My imperial kitten!' to which the Duchess retorts, 'Imperial Fiddlesticks!' If you are lucky enough to have an imperial or even an imperious kitten, Lily could be an appropriate name.

Lincoln It was President Abraham Lincoln who first introduced a cat into the White House. He was known to be extremely fond of cats.

WHO'S <u>REALLY</u> RUNNING THE CITY

Drawing by H. Martin; © *1991 The New Yorker Magazine, Inc.*

Linford After Linford Christie, Olympic 100-metre gold medallist – for the cat with an amazing turn of speed!

Lionel For a cat that's dark, sleek and very affectionate.

Livingstone I presume . . . The famous doctor who spent a lot of time in Africa, discovering places and documenting his travels. For the adventurous cat.

Lolita A youthful temptress in the novel of the same name by Vladimir Nabokov. For the kitten-cat who seduces you from the start.

Lothario 'Is this the haughty, gallant, gay Lothario?' Nicholas Rowe's famous seducer of women from *The Fair Penitent*. A name to live up to.

Lottie Short for Charlotte, the resourceful spider in the delightful children's book later made into an animated film, *Charlotte's Web*.

Lucy, Lucille, Lucinda, Luz These names are all derived from the Latin word *lux*, meaning 'light'. For those who light up your life.

M

Mabel A name derived from the Latin word *amabilis* meaning 'lovable'. Diminutive forms are Mab and Mabs.

Macaulay A distinguished name not to be used frivolously. Namesakes include Catherine, radical historian; Dame Rose, novelist and travel writer; and Thomas Babington, politician and historian.

Machiavelli With an obvious diminutive, this makes reference to Niccolò Machiavelli (1469–1527), the Italian political theorist and writer whose name has become synonymous with political intrigue. A cat with an evil streak, perhaps.

Mac/Mack For the computer cat. Also an affectionate name for an older mouser, akin to 'mate' or 'buddy'.

Mackenzie Sir Compton Mackenzie was a Scottish author perhaps best known for his riotous book *Whisky Galore*. For the cat with a penchant for kilts.

Madonna A contrary name, perhaps for a much revered cat who nevertheless shamelessly flaunts her sexuality.

Mae The type of cat that might purr, 'Come up and see me sometime.' Definitely a bedroom type of cat.

Malfi The desire of a widowed duchess to marry beneath her position is cruelly thwarted by her brothers in John Webster's *The Duchess of Malfi* (1614). For the pedigreed puss who lusts after the tabby down the road.

Mansell After the British racing car driver Nigel Mansell – for the cat that keeps tearing around (and around and around) the room at breakneck speed.

Manx A tailless variety of cat.

Mao After Mao Tse-Tung (1893–1976), a fearless swimmer and one of the founders of the Chinese Communist Party. For revolutionary cats.

Marmalade An old favourite for a fluffy ginger cat.

Mars Roman god of war and the fourth planet from the sun. For a bellicose cat, a red cat or one that's just from another planet.

Martha Sister of Lazarus and Mary Magdalene, Martha is the patron saint of housewives. Not a name for the liberated feline, but if your cat is somewhat old-fashioned, then Martha is a saintly name for her.

Matilda Like **Jemima**, Matilda seems to be rather a haughty name. It was introduced by the Normans, and there were several queens of that name. It is a compound of 'might', 'strength', 'battle' and 'strife': a somewhat belligerent name.

Maudred Old-fashioned name for an old-fashioned cat.

Maurice *See* **Doris**.

Mazuma Slang for 'money'. Appropriate for an expensive, exotic cat.

Mazurka After the Polish dance. A beautiful name for a long-furred, foreign female.

Medusa For a cat with a stony glare.

Mehitabel The name of a wise and sophisticated little cat whose friend and confidant was a cockroach named Archy.

Meriwether The third of three sprites in Walt Disney's version of *Sleeping Beauty*. *See* **Fauna**, **Flora**.

Merry For your carefree, cheerful, convivial, comical, carousing cat, especially if it has entered your life at a festive time of year.

Mikado A lovely name for an oriental mouser. Brings to mind the much-loved opera written by Gilbert and Sullivan in 1885.

Millamant Congreve's Millamant in *The Way of the World* was one of the first champions of feminism. It was Millamant who said, 'A little disdain is not amiss; a little scorn is alluring,' and how well that could describe an Abyssinian beauty.

Minerva The Roman goddess of wisdom.

Ming One of the most famous dynasties of China (1368–1644). For a fine porcelain cat.

Minnaloushe The underworld connection again. This was a black cat immortalized by Irish poet W.B. Yeats, who was widely known to have been fascinated by the occult. This cat is described as 'the nearest kin of the moon'.

Miranda The daughter of Prospero in Shakespeare's *The Tempest*. Her name means 'to be wondered at'.

Misfit When no other name will do.

Miss Puss Dick Whittington's cat, otherwise known as Cat, from the fairy tale by Andrew Lang, *Dick Whittington and His Cat*. A memorial has been built in her memory on Highgate Hill, London.

Mr Magoo A short-sighted cartoon character who frequently bumps into things. A good name for a clumsy cat.

Mr Tibbs Sidney Poitier's three Mr Tibbs detective films made this name famous. If your feline friend is something of a sleuth, look no further.

Mitzi A popular name for the family mouser. Also appropriate for the cat with a touch of glamour, like Hollywood star Mitzi Gaynor.

Mocha A fine-quality coffee originally from Yemen, where the region known as Mocha is situated. Can denote a rich coffee/chocolate colouring.

Mog After Mog the cat from the classic children's 'Meg and Mog' picture books by Jan Piénkowski.

Moggie Short for Mogadon – for a lazy, sleepy cat!

Mohawk From the name of a tribe of North American Indians. Ideal for the cat with spiky fur.

Molotov A Bolshevik revolutionary. Today, it is best known as a home-made bomb. Pick a volatile cat to suit.

Monroe Marilyn. For the blonde bombshell that believes that diamonds are a cat's best friend.

Mopsy *See* **Flopsy**.

Morgan Perhaps after Morgan le Fay, queen of Avalon and King Arthur's half-sister, who tried ambivalently to kill and cure Arthur. Morgan revealed to Arthur, through a magic draught, the intrigues of his wife Guinevere and Sir Lancelot. For the cat who hides its claws.

Morticia The Gothic wife of Gomez in the cult sixties TV series *The Addams Family*, about a family from the 'dark' side who try to integrate into normal suburban life. Only for the black feline.

Mowcher A Dickensian character, Miss Mowcher was the diminutive hairdresser employed by Steerforth and introduced to David Copperfield. She was quick-witted, observant and sharp.

Mozart Wolfgang Amadeus. A perfect name for the genius cat. And as Mozart was not the most demure of people, the abbreviation of his first name to **Wolfie** should not offend.

Muffin, Muffins A very popular name with children, it would suit a roundly shaped mouser.

Mysouff The pet cat of nineteenth-century French writer Alexandre Dumas. The cat was reputed to have had psychic powers.

N

Nefertiti The Egyptian queen with the famous profile. For cats whose image deserves to be recorded in plaster.

Nellie The gossipy housekeeper in *Wuthering Heights* who recounts the tale of **Heathcliff** and Cathy. For the homey cat that loves to lie on the hearth rug by the fire.

Newton One of Isaac Newton's lesser-known achievements was the invention of the cat-flap. A man any cat would be proud to be named after.

Nicholas The last tsar of Russia. If your cat wanders, name him after the last of the Romanoffs.

Nijinsky Vaslav (1890–1950), one of the most famous Russian dancers and choreographers of all time. Alas, he went mad in 1917 and the world was the poorer. An excellent name for any lithe and graceful cat.

Nile Cats were worshipped in ancient Egypt. Name your cat for the life-giver of Egyptian civilization.

Nina *See* **Antonia**.

Noël Is your cat not at all courageous? Name him for Noël Coward. Also a good name for a kitten given as a gift at Christmas.

O

Octavia A classic Roman name, perhaps the most famous Octavia being Marc Antony's abandoned wife whose charms faded by comparison with **Cleopatra**'s.

Olaf The name of several distinguished Scandinavian kings.

Oliver 'Please, sir, can I have some more?' A famous line from the film *Oliver!*, adapted from the book by Charles Dickens. For the hungry and lonely cat forced into a life of petty theft to survive.

Omar The twelfth-century Persian poet most famous for his poem *The Rubaiyat*. A suitably classic name for a pedigree Persian cat.

Omega The last letter in the Greek alphabet and a name that signifies the last in a series.

Onassis Short and slick; a good name for a ship's cat.

Orlando Orlando, the Marmalade Cat, is the hero of a classic series of picture books by Kathleen Hale, first published in 1938. Orlando and his wife **Grace** are accompanied by kittens **Pansy**, the tortoiseshell, the white **Blanche** and coal-black **Tinkle**.

Orson According to fable, Orson and his twin brother
  Valentine were born in a wood near Orleans,
  where Orson was taken by a bear and suckled with
  her cubs. He later became the terror of France,
  known as the Wild Man of the Forest. Orson Welles
  fans will be interested to know the origin of the
  name.

Orwell In *Animal Farm* George Orwell wrote, 'All
  animals are equal, but some are more equal than
  others.' For the cat who's a cut above the rest.

Oscar After the flamboyant writer Oscar Wilde –
  perfect for the cat that loves to show off.

Osiris Husband of **Isis** and Egyptian god of the
  underworld. A mystical name for a serious cat.

Ottoline An amorous cat in memory of Lady Ottoline
  Morrell, a literary figure who had many lovers.

Otto Prince Otto von Bismarck, if you prefer to use his
  full title. Use it for your pedigreed Prussian.

P

Pansy *See* **Orlando**.

Pavarotti Only suitable for the LARGE cat with a voice to match!

Pearl A rare and valued feline, especially apt for the maternal cat: Mother-of-Pearl.

Pebbles Fred and Wilma's daughter from *The Flintstones*. For the cat that tracks litter through the house.

Pedro Emperor of Brazil. Perfect for the coffee-coloured cat.

Pepper For the speedy mouser with unusual markings or little black flecks through his fur.

Percival According to some versions, Percival, Knight of the Round Table, found the Holy Grail. A somewhat archaic name well suited to that Middle-Aged cat.

Perdita Meaning 'lost' in Latin, this would be a good name for a rescued stray.

Periwinkle The greater and lesser periwinkle are evergreen trailing shrubs with light-blue starry flowers. The name is also applied to small blue molluscs found on the seashore.

Pharaoh Literally 'great house', so be sure of your feline's lineage before you bestow this title.

Phoebe Means 'shining one' – the name the ancient Greeks gave to the goddess of the moon. According to legend, Phoebe was a Titan, daughter of Heaven and Earth.

Phuket For the Siamese cat who takes its holidays at Club Med.

Piaf French slang for 'sparrow'. Also the surname chosen by legendary singer Edith Piaf, who was only 4 feet 10 inches tall. For the very small and fragile cat.

Picasso After the Spanish painter well known for his Blue Period, this would be an appropriate name for a Siamese blue.

Pickles For the puss that is constantly getting into a jam.

Pierrot An inspired name for a black-and-white cat, especially a very thin one, looking rather like a sad clown. If he had a mate, the obvious name for her would be **Pierrette**.

Pinkle Purr *See* **Tattoo**.

Pip Short for Philip, as in Charles Dickens's character Philip Pirrip in *Great Expectations*.

Pitti Sing One of the three little maids from school from *The Mikado* by Gilbert and Sullivan.

Pixie A light-footed cat with magical presence.

Platypus For a cat that's unusually fond of water.

Prince This is a dignified name for a pedigreed cat. It would also suit the cat with a penchant for purple if named after pop superstar Prince.

Pushkin A lovely onomatopoeic moniker with distinctly Russian associations – Aleksandr Pushkin was a distinguished writer of the nineteenth century. **Pushka** (Russian for 'cannon') would suit his wife.

Puss From the children's pantomine *Puss 'n Boots* and the nursery rhyme:

> Pussy Cat, Pussy Cat, where have you been?
> I've been to London to visit the Queen.

Q

Queenie A very popular name that came into favour in the early years of Queen Victoria's reign. It became a tribute to the highest feminine qualities.

R

Rambo A savage mouser would suit this name, which has become synonymous with an image of a sweaty soldier of fortune.

Rameses An ancient Egyptian king. A suitably regal name for a sleek and dignified cat.

Regina Somewhat regal, as the name means 'queen', but it can be shortened to Reggie for that slow-moving, languid cat.

Rhapsody Meaning a grandiloquent piece of music, this name would suit a cat that likes to do things on a grand scale. Also brings to mind the much-admired jazz concerto *Rhapsody in Blue* by George Gershwin.

Rhubarb A popular choice for the family favourite. Could denote a rather ruddy coat. In *Rhubarb*, an American film, made in 1951, an alley cat named Rhubarb inherits $30 million and a major-league baseball club.

Rochester If your cat is large and dark or hides a secret, then name him after Charlotte Brontë's hero, Mr Rochester, in *Jane Eyre*.

Rocky For a fighter that claws his way to the top.

Rococo A lush style of decoration from eighteenth-century Europe, appropriate for a flamboyant feline.

Rodin The thinking person's cat.

Rolls Name your cat for the Rolls-Royce engine if he's got a smooth, quiet purr.

Romeo From Shakespeare's immortal *Romeo and Juliet*. The name has since developed connotations of insincere flattery and seduction, so if your cat is a heartbreaker, this name would suit.

Roxanne The meaning of this name, which is also found as Roxana and Roshana, is 'dawn of day'. The name has recently been revived and popularized as the title of both a movie and a song.

Rudi For the cat with a balletic turn of leap.

Rusty This is a very popular name, often denoting a reddish hue to a cat's fur.

S

Saffron A spice used for its distinctive orange colouring, from the Arabic *zafaran*. An imaginative alternative for your orange cat.

Sage For a feline that is greenish-grey, like the healing herb, or for the cat who seems judiciously wise, or pretends to be.

Salami An irreverent name for a sausage-shaped cat.

Samba An erotic Brazilian dance – only if your cat is a full-blooded, passionate Carioca.

Santa Claws: a Christmas special.

Satchmo Meaning Satchel Mouth, after the famous jazz trumpet player Louis 'Satchmo' Armstrong. For a voracious but friendly cat.

Sathan/Satan A cat that appeared in the Chelmsford witchcraft trials of 1579. An appropriate name if your pet is black with pointy ears and tail.

Scipio To ensure that there is no disrespect to the noble Roman general, we should change the spelling of this name to Skippio. For cats that proceed by leaps and bounds.

Scroobious Pip From Edward Lear's poem – all the beasts in the world try to place a mysterious creature that insists its only name is Scroobious Pip. For that unique cat.

Sebastian The elegant down-and-out hero of Waugh's *Brideshead Revisited*. Reminiscent of a golden, decadent time, your cat should have all the faded splendour of the English aristocracy.

Sekhmet This Egyptian goddess was the 'Great Cat'. Her influence is wholly good, and, as one would expect, she is linked with the moon. A very special, awe-inspiring name.

Sergeant Tibs The cat in *101 Dalmatians* by Dodie Smith.

Sersa If you like **Xerxes** but feel that the lofty name is likely to cause embarrassment, why not choose Sersa as a simpler version? It is also a pretty name.

Shabbottey An amusing and interesting name for a cat. It comes originally from *Chat Botté* – the booted cat, 'Puss 'n Boots' in fact.

Shadow For the blackest black cat that likes to follow you around.

She Or, in full, 'She-Who-Must-be-Obeyed'. The terrifying queen in the Rider Haggard novel *She*. Obviously for the cat that rules the hearth.

Sherlock After Sherlock Holmes, the famous British detective. If you have a pair of inquisitive kittens, consider calling them **Holmes** and **Watson**.

Sherry Originally, white fortified wine made in Spain at Jerez de la Frontera. Sherry is suitable for cats with a variety of colours, from the pale dry to smooth dark brown.

Si One of the devious pair of Siamese cats in *Lady and the Tramp*, a Disney film. **Am** is the other villain.

Sibyl Cats are mysterious, and so were the sibyls of Roman mythology. They were prophetesses who lived to a great age and who were models of female intellectual beauty.

Simon The oldest pet forms of this name are Symond, Symkyn and Simpkin. The tailor's cat in Beatrix Potter's *Tailor of Gloucester* was called Simpkin.

Sinh A cat with golden eyes that was worshipped in Burma by a sect of priests who believed it had oracular powers. Perfect for the Burmese pet.

Sistrum In ancient times this was a metal rattle, used especially in the worship of Isis. On the upper bend of the instrument there was usually a carving of a cat's head, often with a human face.

Sisyphus Mythical figure of Greek legend whose punishment was a lifetime of impossible tasks. Good name for a cat whose repetitive behaviour appears to be futile.

Skindleshanks A railway cat made famous by T. S. Eliot. No train could leave without him.

Skittle For the skittish kitten that often sends things flying.

Smarty For the cat with a high IQ who is sometimes a little big for his boots.

Somerled *See* **Torquil**.

Snap Snap, crackle and pop! Ideal names for a playful trio.

Snark From *The Hunting of the Snark* by Lewis Carroll. Be sure your cat is bizarre enough to compete with Carroll's mythological creature.

Socks A perennial favourite revitalized in the Nineties by US President Clinton's cat.

Sooty and **Sweep** These teddy bear- and dog-puppets were created in the 1950s by Harry Corbett and are still favourites. Both would suit a black cat.

Sophia A name recalling the voluptuous Italian actress Sophia Loren. Your feline would have to have an hourglass figure.

Soraya The name of the first wife of the late Shah of Iran. Soraya was sad, lonely and beautiful. A good name for an imperious Persian.

Sorrel For a bright chestnut-coloured cat.

Sphinx The Egyptian Sphinx was a lion, usually with a pharaoh's head, symbolizing royal power. This name would lend itself to a mysterious and powerful feline. *See* **Giza**.

Spider For the long-legged cat.

Spike After Spike Milligan – for the slightly nutty cat.

Steffi After the tennis player Steffi Graf – a good name for the cat that pounces on its hapless prey with lightning speed.

Stella Means 'star' in Latin. The name was used by Sir Philip Sidney, who wrote sonnets and songs collectively titled *Astrophel and Stella*.

Stephen After thriller writer Stephen King, whose films incude *Cat's Eyes*, in which a cat becomes involved in some very bizarre situations.

Stevie   Oh, I am a cat that likes to
                Gallop about doing good.

But unfortunately Stevie Smith gave no name to the jolly good-natured creature described in her poem *The Galloping Cat*. Might we not then call a cat with such an agreeable disposition Stevie?

Sullivan *See* **Gilbert**.

Sundae A treat for every day of the week.

Sweep *See* **Sooty**.

Sydney Why not name your cat after this beautiful Australian city? One thing you can be certain of, Sydney will never be dull.

Sylvester The black-and-white cartoon cat that splutters when he talks and is forever tormenting the poor little canary Tweetie Pie.

T

T'ang Dynasty of China (618–907). Well suited to the oriental breed.

Tabasco The perfect name for a saucy cat with a red-hot temper.

Tabitha The comfortable cat, as depicted by Beatrix Potter.

Tama A popular name in Japan for a cat, it means 'jewel'.

Tarot If your cat has unexplainable powers and can foretell the future, name it after the tarot-card pack.

Tatters and **Rags** Apt names for a scraggly-looking pair.

Tattoo   Tattoo was the mother of Pinkle Purr,
A little black nothing of feet and fur;

Christopher Milne, son of A.A. Milne and the model for Christopher Robin in the Pooh books, recalling his favourite cat.

Teazle In Sheridan's *The School for Scandal* Lady Teazle was a charming, lovable coquette, flirtatious but fundamentally faithful to a husband twice her age.

Tess, Tessa For the rags-to-riches (and back to rags again) type of cat, after the heroine of Thomas Hardy's novel *Tess of the D'Urbervilles*.

Thatcher Margaret Thatcher, former British Prime Minister, gained fame, originally, for depriving English children of their government-subsidized milk. Name your cat for her if she runs up large milk bills.

Thomasina Heroine of a novel by Paul Gallico, later filmed as *Three Lives of Thomasina*, in which the feline heroine recovers from three crises, to the joy of her young mistress.

Tibby Short for Tibert, the cat who appeared in *Reynard the Fox*. *See* **Tibert**, **Tybalt**, **Tybert**.

Tiberius An imposing name for an imposing creature. Can be shortened to the more friendly Tiber.

Tibert, Tybalt, Tybert The French form of Gilbert, this is a traditional name for cats. Tibert is the cat in *Reynard the Fox*, and Shakespeare uses the reference for his character in *Romeo and Juliet* – Mercutio addresses Tybalt as a 'rat-catcher' and 'Good King of Cats!' *See* **Gib**.

Tiddles From the old English slang to indulge, nurse and cherish. For those pampered pets.

Tiger Not only will this name refer to the markings on your cat, but he will also have a wild streak.

Tigger The lovable but incorrigible tiger in *Winnie the Pooh* whose bounce and bravado get him into all sorts of scrapes. For the amiable and adventurous cat.

Tiggy Abbreviation of either **Tigger** or **Tiger**.

Tina After the raunchy rock star Tina Turner – for the cat with a screamer of a voice!

Tinkle *See* **Orlando**.

Titania In Shakespeare's *A Midsummer Night's Dream*, Titania is the wife of Oberon and Queen of the Fairies. For the bewitching cat that casts a spell over you.

Tolstoy A distinguished name. Leo Tolstoy (1828–1910) was the world-famous Russian writer whose works include *War and Peace* and *Anna Karenina*.

Tom A male cat. The name was popularized by the Tom and Jerry cartoons, about a cat and mouse who are sometimes friends, usually enemies.

Tonic *See* **Gin**.

Tony Broadway's highest award. For the dramatic cat.

Torquil It is sometimes very difficult to trace a name back to its first usage. For example, Torquil and Somerled, very fine names, have long been considered as Scottish. Unusual and gracious.

Drawing by M. Stevens; © 1991 The New Yorker Magazine, Inc.

Tortilla A Mexican cat that adds a bit of spice to your life.

Toscanini Arturo Toscanini. Famous Italian conductor. Great for the cat who leads the feline chorus.

Toulouse After the wonderful but tragic French painter Henri de Toulouse-Lautrec. *See* **Duchess**.

Towser Reputed by *The Guinness Book of Records* to be history's best mouser, catching an estimated 28,899 mice during her lifetime, an average of three a day.

Trevor Trev is the pet form. For the down-to-earth cat who takes life as it comes.

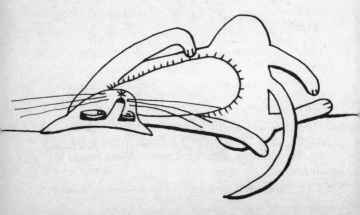

Tristan And **Isolde**. Medieval love poem involving potions, madness and fatal devotion. For star-crossed feline lovers.

Tudor The name of English sovereigns from Henry VII to Elizabeth I. Should only be bestowed upon cats with impeccably royal lineage.

Tutankhamun The youngest of the Pharaoh kings to die, Tutankhamun was embalmed, in accordance with the ancient Egyptian custom. Easily shortened to the more manageable Tut.

Twain Mark Twain's *Notebook* (1935), published posthumously, recalls the comment 'If man could be crossed with the cat it would improve man, but it would deteriorate the cat.'

Twiggy For the doe-eyed model cat that is as skinny as a rake.

Twitcher Who but a cat could be called Twitcher? Jemmy Twitcher, the highwayman in Gay's *Beggar's Opera*, was described as cunning and treacherous.

Typhoon The name for a tropical cyclone or hurricane of the western Pacific or the China Sea. Literally, from the Chinese for Great Wind – Tai Fung. For the little whirlwind who wreaks havoc in your house.

U

Ulanova The Russian ballerina Galina Ulanova. For your Russian Blue who is light on her toes.

Uluru For a red Abyssinian.

Uriel Uriel was one of the seven Old Testament archangels and, according to Milton (in *Paradise Lost*), was the 'Regent of the Sun' and 'sharpest sighted spirit of all in heaven'.

Utopia A Latin essay by Saint Thomas More published in 1516 about the search for the best possible form of government. Today it refers to absolute and ideal future. For the cat that is perfect in every way.

U Nu Burma's first Prime Minister after independence. A good name for a male Burmese.

V

Valentine Romantic associations aside, *see* **Orson**. Also one of Shakespeare's *Two Gentlemen of Verona*, whose serving-man is named Speed.

Valentino For the hot Latin lover who has his pick of the felines on your street. Brings to mind Hollywood superstar and seducer Rudolph Valentino.

Varuna In Hindu mythology Varuna was one of two virtuous sons of Aditi, the Earth Mother. A spirit of the night in the orbit of the moon. He appears as one riding on a sea monster and from his exalted position orders the seasons and controls the rains.

Velvet A fitting name for the Burmese pet with the softest, sleekest fur.

Venus The Roman goddess of love and the second planet from the sun. For the great beauty with a place high in your affections.

Vesuvius For the cat whose eruptions can be violent.

Violet These lightweight flower names are suitable for cats and generally pleasing. Violets are associated with shyness and modesty, the white ones with innocence, the purple ones with faithful love.

Vivaldi Antonio (1675–1741). This name is in honour of the much-loved baroque composer who wrote the *Four Seasons*.

Vogue The magazine. When no other name will do for your style-conscious feline who likes to strike a pose.

Voltaire Pseudonym used by François-Marie Arouet (1694–1778), the French satirist, novelist, dramatist, poet and historian. For the cat that thumbs its nose at the establishment.

W

Waffle A cat without substance but sweet none the less. Would be great for a cat with cross-hatched markings.

Warlock This name means 'doing the work of the devil'. Only if you are not afraid of things that go bump in the night.

Washington This name originally derives from the English village of the same name. It is more famous, though, through George, father of his country.

Watson *See* **Sherlock**.

Wendy A theatre name invented by James Barrie for one of the Darling children in *Peter Pan*.

Whiskers For the cat with brand loyalty.

Whisky The 'spiritous liquor' originally distilled in Ireland and Scotland. In rare usage it can also mean 'light', 'lively' and 'flighty', an apt description of how one feels after a drop of whisky.

Whisper For the quiet, graceful cat that moves silently around the house.

Whitney After Whitney Housten, the American singer famous for her soulful love songs. Ideal for a very beautiful and sensuous cat.

Wilfred Comes from the Anglo-Saxon words for 'will' and 'peace'. The short form is Wilf.

Wilma Wife of Fred and mother of Pebbles, the voice of reason in the Flintstone's Stone Age household.

William Charles Dickens called his cat William, but quickly changed its name to Williamina when it gave birth to kittens.

Willow Although its origins are obscure, this word is associated with sorrow, as in weeping willow. It would suit a slender and melancholy cat.

Winifred Means 'friend of peace'. In the first century AD, St Winifred was beheaded because she refused to marry Prince Caradoc. The usual pet forms are Win, Winnie and Freda.

Winnie A homely name and the nickname of wartime British politician Winston Churchill. Also a great name for a cuddly pussycat that brings to mind Christopher Robin's Winnie the Pooh.

Wolfie *See* **Mozart**.

Wonton Chinese dumpling, eaten with soup. A good name for your rotund pet.

Woodbine Earthy and wholesome-sounding, it is the common name of the wild honeysuckle. Use it for an untamed kitten.

X

Xavier After not Francis Xavier but Xavier Cugat. A good name for a remote, musical cat.

Xerox A good name for a copycat.

Xerxes The King of Persia, defeated at Salamis by Themistocles.

Y

Yang *See* **Yin**.

Yankee New York baseball team, the 'Bronx Bombers'. If you have nine or ten cats, you could name them for the whole team!

Yenta Wonderful name for the cat who can't mind her own business.

Yin In Chinese philosophy, one of the two principles of the universe. It represents the feminine, passive side, while the other, **Yang**, represents the active, assertive side. These would be great names for a pair of opposites.

Yum Yum Another of the three little maids from school in *The Mikado* by Gilbert and Sullivan.

Yvette A sophisticated French name. It would probably suit a Persian or other pampered breed.

Z

Zadoc From Dryden's satire *Absalom and Achitophel*. Zadoc was a priest whose 'lowly mind advanced to David's grace'.

Zelda Wife of F. Scott Fitzgerald. If your cat is extravagant and emotional, here's the name for her.

Zephyr Babar the elephant's little monkey friend was called Zephyr. Zephyr is also a soft, gentle breeze.

Ziggy Cartoon character, or Ziggy Stardust, David Bowie's *alter ego*. For a cat that's alternately comical and musical.

Zingaro The Italian name for a gypsy. This name is for the cat who likes to travel and who can predict the future with its crystal ball.

Zoë From the Greek, meaning 'life'. For that 'little bundle of joy', perhaps a new kitten.

Zola Emile, the leading figure of the French school of naturalistic fiction during the nineteenth century.

Zuleika Not only Max Beerbohm's fascinating heroine
  Zuleika Dobson but also reputedly the name of
  Potiphar's wife, who brought so much trouble to the
  innocent Joseph. The name is frequently found in
  Persian poetry, so it would be an appropriate name
  for a Persian kitten.

OTHER TITLES IN THE SERIES

Tips and Techniques for Microwave Cooking
How to Remove Stains
How to Make Over 200 Cocktails
Choosing Baby Names
Chess Made Easy
Family First Aid
Choosing Dog Names
Transform Your Public Speaking
The Pocket Easy Speller